Napoleon
1769 - 1821

Priya Mani

Prodigy

Napoleon

First Edition: December 2009
80 Pages
Printed in India.

ISBN 978–81–8493–290–4
Pro–ya–en–54

Prodigy Books
177/103, First Floor, Ambal's Building
Lloyds Road, Royapettah, Chennai 600 014.
Ph: +91-44-4200-9603
Email: support@nhm.in
Website: www.nhm.in

Prodigy Books is an imprint of New Horizon Media Pvt. Ltd.

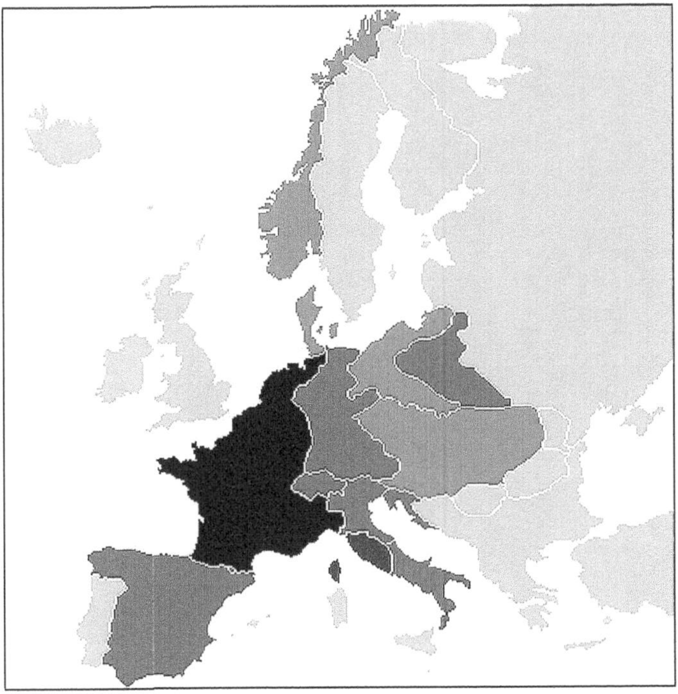

First French Empire at its greatest extent in 1811

French Empire

Conquered "Rebellious" States

Conquered "Allied" States

Chapter 1

Ting Tong. At the sound of the doorbell, Anitha set down the casserole she was scrubbing and quickly washed her hands under the tap. Wiping her hands on the pallu of her saree, Mom came out of the kitchen to answer the call.

It was her twelve-year old daughter, Vaishali, just back from school.

"Vaishu, back home so soon? How was your day at school?"

No response. Instead, Vaishali flung her shoes in a corner, and tossed her satchel of books by the showcase before slumping on the sofa.

Anitha sighed. "Ok, wash your hands and face and come for lunch, dear. I will lay the table."

This was the fourth day in succession when Vaishali had come from school, morose and aloof.

Over the meal, Vaishali opened up. "I am not going to the school anymore, Mom. They keep calling me all sorts of names - Shorty, Pigmy, Lilliput, Thumbelina. I have had enough."

"Oh, is that the matter? I should have known better. Come on, Vaishu, how long are you going to take offence for such little things?"

Now Vaishali was a really cute-looking girl - fair complexioned, round-eyed with dainty lips. Her eyelashes were doll-like, ebony and long, to match her hair; and cheeks that turned crimson at the slightest prod. But she had a tiny regret - that she was short, in fact a little too short for girls her age. Now, while it was nice being cute, it was not always nice being short.

Being short meant not being taken seriously by friends and peers. Being short meant missing the better part of most cultural programmes, unless one made a dash for that seat in the front. Being short meant being constantly made fun of by taller classmates; who spared no opportunity to remind you what a queer little creature you were.

Vaishali was not new to this experience. And what she lacked in height, she made up with a superabundance of talent. For, Vaishali was a bright student; proficient not just in academics, but most extracurricular activities as well. To start with, she had a sweet voice. And when she danced, she was graceful and lithe. Her genius lay in debates and dramatics, in which she was equalled by few. Only that, her classmates did not know what a bundle of talent Vaishali was; her new classmates at Carmel Convent School, Pondicherry.

Following an official transfer from Pune, Vaishali's father had moved in that summer to Pondicherry with his family. And so it was that Vaishali had to leave old friends and classmates behind to find herself new ones in an unfamiliar place.

It would be altogether unfair to say that the students of Carmel Convent School were unfriendly to the newcomer. In fact, the boisterous batch of 7th grade, section C were so taken on by the barbie-like Vaishali that they began to amuse themselves with her as if she were a doll, rather than a new classmate, who should be gently made to feel at home in a new environment. Some pulled her cheeks, while the others found her 'tiny' and 'cute'. The more bold ones, however, found irrepressible glee in calling her by names like 'elfin', 'pixie', 'short stuff' and 'thumbelina'. And all this disconcerted the sensitive Vaishali, who did not relish this relentless reference to her lack of height.

"It is not funny, Mom. I am sick and tired of it all," she cried. Mom realized something had to be done.

The very next morning, Vaishali's parents went to the school to meet her class teacher. She patiently heard them out; then assured them that she'd do the needful for their precious daughter. When Vaishali's parents left, the teacher sat on her desk for a while, in pensive thought. Suddenly, her brow cleared. Gathering her books, she rose from her desk; and in a crisp stride, made a beeline to the last classroom on the right end of the corridor, the classroom of 7th grade, section C.

Nandana Balakrishnan, taught English and History to the higher classes. Her flair for language was unsurpassed. Her gift of narration was such that a boring history lesson became a lively experience. She was, by large, a role model for the students. They loved her voice, her poise and were smitten by her style and self-assurance. The youngsters looked forward to her classes, and even vied with each other to be in her good books. So when Miss Krishnan walked into the sprightly class of 7 C, fifty bright voices greeted her with a booming "Good Morning Miss."

"Good Morning, Class. Sit Down. Today, I shall not be taking any lessons. Instead..."

An instantaneous uproar rent the air. Jubilant cries of 'Hurray' and 'Yahoo' were heard across the classroom. Miss Krishnan thumped the duster on the table twice to make herself heard above the deafening noise.

"Behave yourselves, girls. I haven't even completed," she said, as the girls settled down, half murmuring, half resentful, of the celebration snipped mid-way.

When silence reigned once more, Miss Krishnan continued, "Our school is hosting the French Festival next month in collaboration with Alliance Francaise of Pondicherry. It is going to be a grand affair, a riot of sounds and colours. We will be presenting an exhibition on the life and times of the French people across the ages. There will be screening of acclaimed French films. We have even planned a ballet on the life of Napoleon Bonaparte. The whole idea behind this cultural extravaganza is to showcase the rich and exuberant culture of the French people. And remember, schools in and around Pondicherry will be invited too."

"And what about food stalls?"

"Of course. What is French culture without its cuisine?" Miss Krishnan replied. Then continued, "Now coming to the point. In lieu of this forthcoming French fiesta, I thought it would be interesting to suspend our regular lessons for a while, and take up the life of Napoleon Bonaparte instead.

Not only would it give you all a fair idea of this towering personality of French, in fact, world history; it would also be an orientation exercise for those of you, who are lucky enough to be selected for the ballet. Any questions?"

There were none.

Chapter 2

"Let me take you all to Corsica, the fourth largest island in the Mediterranean Sea, located south-east of France. Endowed with the luxuriance of mountains, natural forests and rivers, this ravishing island has earned for itself the epithet, 'The Isle of Beauty'.

"On the west coast of this island is Ajaccio, its capital city and home to 'Casa Buonaparte', the ancestral mansion of the Buonapartes. The Buonapartes..."

A hand went up. "You mean, the Bonapartes, miss?"

"Well, I mean, the Buonapartes, at least to begin with. For, the Buonapartes were primarily minor Italian gentry who had immigrated to Corsica in the 16th century. So you can see the heavy Italian influence even in their names. Our hero too was born as Napoleone di Buonaparte on the 15th of August, 1769 to Nobile Carlo Buonaparte and Maria Letizia Ramolino Buonaparte; although he later embraced the more French-like name, Napoleon Bonaparte."

"But why would he change his name so?" Praveena interrupted.

"A string of circumstances. To start with, Napoleon was born at a time when Corsica was witnessing a sweeping national antagonism against the French. And naturally too. Corsica was a sovereign nation, who had gained national independence from Genoa in 1755. When she was in her thirteenth year of sovereignty, France attempted to subjugate her again, by secretly purchasing Corsica from the Republic of Genoa. There was a brief war between the two in 1768-69, by which France established her supremacy over the Corsican island, just three months before Napoleon's birth. This was a predominant French influence that stalked Napoleon, not just at the time of his birth but, in fact, even his growing years."

"Excuse me miss," Samprada's hand went up, "But this sort of an event could only have sparked in Napoleon, a lasting hatred for anything French. How does it justify the subsequent change of name?"

"Well, it had to do with the social status of the Buonapartes. The Buonapartes qualified as well-off Corsican nobility in the eyes of the local inhabitants. But the fact was, their affluence did not match up to the standards of aristocratic grandeur elsewhere, say in France. It was definitely not so for Carlo Buonaparte, who had the uphill task of raising eight children within his limited means."

"Eight children?" came a whoosh of astonishment from the class.

"Yes. Napoleon was only the second child of his parents, the first being Giuseppe (later Joseph) Buonaparte. Among his younger siblings were three sisters - Elisa, Paoletta (later Pauline) and Caroline and three brothers - Lucien, Luigi (later Louis) and Girolamo (later Jerome)."

"The lessons of strength and courage came early to this penny-pinched family. Mother Letizia, the stout disciplinarian trained her children early on to suffer hardships and yet not show it out. But how long could one live in penury and wretchedness? And why would one endure poverty when there were other by-lanes to prosperity?"

"Father Carlo, an attorney who had participated in the Corsican war of independence, came to a drastic decision. He made a shocking change of allegiance. In other words, he switched his loyalties. Corsica, his country was in the throes of an anti-French upheaval. But Carlo Buonaparte decided to embrace the French rule."

"Carlo Buonaparte worked his way to power under the French to become, in 1777, a count and Corsica's representative in the court of Louis XVI, the then King of France. It was an astute strategy of political opportunism. It gave Carlo the right connections to get his son Napoleon educated in France."

"Do you realize, girls, how destiny is steering the young Napoleon towards France?"

"Yes, miss," came the vibrant chorus, in response.

"A thin, pale boy of nine years, thus, stepped into France for the first time in 1778. A new comer in a new land, much like our young Vaishali here," at which forty-nine pair of eyes turned to look at her. Vaishali reddened with embarrassment.

"Napoleon was first admitted to a school in Autun to learn French. Later, in May 1799, he was taken in at the military academy at Brienne-le-Chateau. Life at the academy was not easy for this young Corsican, who was mocked and disdained by his schoolmates as an uncouth foreigner. The lonely lad, however, applied himself to his studies and even distinguished himself in mathematics, history and geography."

"Five years later, in 1784, Napoleon was promoted to the Ecole Militaire, the royal military school in Paris. Here, he was tutored in the science of artillery. Tragedy struck, however, with Carlo Buonaparte's death in February 1785. In a single moment, Napoleon found himself threatened again with poverty."

A hush came over the class at this unexpected turn of events. A meek voice finally found the words to ask, "Did he have to discontinue his studies, miss?"

"Quite the contrary. Do you know what Napoleon did? Instead of losing hope and heart, Napoleon steeled himself, put his soul into his studies and completed the prescribed two-year course in a single year! And in September 1785, at the tender age of sixteen, Napoleon graduated as a second lieutenant of one of the finest artillery regiments of the French army."

At this, the school bell rang. Miss Krishnan gathered her books and walked out of the classroom, leaving a bunch of fifty students in awestruck silence.

Chapter 3

It was the first period after lunch, the sleepiest hour of the afternoon, but the class of 7C were, however, wide awake. It was Nandana Krishnan's class, and she was narrating an interesting story. What more could one ask for?

Miss Krishnan arrived and resumed the account of Napoleon's life.

"1789 is a crucial year in world history. It was also a turning point in Napoleon's destiny. For ,1789 was the year of the French Revolution."

"What sparked off the Revolution, miss?" That was Vaishali. A vague sympathy, shall we say, a fellow feeling had sprung in her heart for Napoleon. Here was someone who had faced the 'unfriendliness' of an alien country at a tender age of nine, yet surmounted all odds to chart the course of world history. Naturally, she was curious to learn more about his fate.

"Plenty of reasons. The first and foremost was the unequal socio-economic structure that prevailed in France. It was called The Old Regime. It segregated its citizens in Three Estates on the basis of their class and rank. The First Estate was the Church or the clergy who, despite owning ten percent of the land, paid no tax. The Second Estate was comprised of the nobility or the landed gentry. They formed only two percent of the population, but owned twenty percent of the land, and enjoyed seventy percent of the wealth. These were people who led grandiose lifestyles at the cost of the Third Estate."

"The Third Estate?"

"Yes, the commoners; the impoverished majority of the populace who bore the brunt of the financial burden that the aristocrats had placed on them. In this category fell:

a) the middle class - professionals, merchants and craftsmen

b) the agricultural peasants, who were virtually at the mercy of the land-owning gentry

c) the working poor, the worst hit in the country

The peasants and the working class had been discontented with their monarch for a long while. To begin with, France had been constantly warring with fellow countries because of which her economy had taken a severe beating. The national resources were being steadily depleted for the wars, and there was a parallel rise in unemployment. If this weren't enough, the country faced a string of successive crop failures. All these heightened the woes of the poor peasants who were driven to the brink of starvation. Even a single meal a day was a luxury to these downtrodden citizens. But stone-blind to their distressing plight, the ruler and his gentry, instead, imposed on them higher taxes."

The class sat in rapt attention, arrested by the atrocious misdeeds of an unsympathetic king.

"Economic crisis was not the only cause of the spectacular showdown of 1789. France was also witnessing, at this time, the rise of the middle class or the bourgeoisie."

"The bourgeoisie were deeply influenced by the thinkers of the Enlightenment, particularly by Voltaire, the French Enlightenment thinker. He inspired among them revolutionary ideas of liberty, equality, fraternity or brotherhood, reason and self-governance. As a result, the country witnessed the emergence of an increasingly intellectual class of people who questioned the unjust taxation policies, state interference into the personal lives of its citizens, even oppression by a despotic ruler. In fact, they questioned the very nature of the divine right of the king."

"What is divine right of the king, miss?"

"It is a politico-religious belief, according to which a ruler derives his powers from the will of God. Since, a ruler receives his powers directly from God, they cannot be questioned by the common man. The king enjoys absolute rights and is the supreme wielder of authority."

"In the name of the divine right, many kings across the breadth of history misused their powers. King Louis XVI, the then ruler of France, was no exception."

"Thus, resentment brewed against the monarch; as well as against the ruling elite classes. People began to clamour for their natural rights, for equality, for the rule of law, and the abolition of the monarchy."

"How could Louis XVI be so immune to the pulse of his people, miss? Didn't he take any measures to address the people's grievances? Or stem the tide of widespread hostility?" The question was popped by Praveena, who could not accept the paradox of a dim-witted autocrat. Despotic rulers needed to be shrewd and crafty to perpetuate their tyranny."

"Well-said, Praveena. In the face of such widespread public antipathy, the ruler had to save his skin, isn't it? King Louis XVI did just that. Anticipating a fearful backlash, he summoned the French Parliament at Versailles in May 1789, for the first time in 150 years! As Louis XVI claimed, it was a move to restructure the taxation policies and bring relief to the poverty-stricken masses through reform."

"Unfortunately for Louis XVI, the Parliament was a miserable failure. The clergy and nobility dominated the talks right from the beginning. Five weeks into the talks, the representatives of the Third Estate realized that the whole affair had been a mere eyewash; that the wealthy and power hungry aristocrats had no intentions of sharing their power or the penury of the masses."

"Indignant at this double-dealing in the hands of the ruling class, the members of the Third Estate left the premises of the Parliament in disgust and reassembled at an indoor tennis court close by. The Third Estate, then, formed a consortium or alliance, along with a few other members of the clergy and nobility. Proclaiming themselves as the National Assembly, the group pledged to stick together until they had given France and its people their rightful constitution. This came to be known as the Tennis Court Oath."

"The failure of the Estates General was the final straw on the camel's back. The Revolution broke out. A furious, hysterical mob stormed the prison of Bastille, the royal fortress that held the prisoners, and set all the convicts free. It was a mighty insurrection (uprising), the first of its kind, challenging the authority of the King. The historic date was July 14, 1789."

"By August 1789, the National Constituent Assembly (the erstwhile National Assembly) adopted the epochal Declaration of the Rights of Man and of the Citizen. The Declaration guaranteed the citizens of France certain indisputable fundamental rights. Equality before law was recognized. The Declaration also stripped the exclusive privileges of the elite gentry, and paved the way for a limited, constitutional monarchy. France was now a democracy."

"So the Revolution lasted only for two months?" asked the surprised Prachi, the regular first-bencher.

"No, Prachi. It lasted much longer. In fact, the years that followed were marked by civil unrest and violent outbreaks all across the country. The infuriated masses were not content with just a few rights. They now raged and thirsted for the blood of the ruling class. The Revolution came to an end in 1792 with the complete dissolution of monarchy. France was declared a sovereign republic. Louis XVI was beheaded. So was his wife, the infamous Marie Antoneitte, nine months later in 1793."

"What followed was one of the bleakest periods in the annals of history. A Reign of Terror unleashed itself on France. The festering wounds of centuries of tyranny and oppression hadn't healed. The mobs found an outlet for their long-suppressed emotions, by directing their brutal fury on the nobles. They sentenced several thousands of individuals associated with the Old Regime to execution by guillotine."

"What was the guillotine, miss?"

"A guillotine was a contraption by which a heavy but sharp blade was brought down with force on a person's neck, thus beheading him."

"But miss, Napoleon doesn't figure at all amidst any of these happenings," cried Samprada, raising her hand.

Almost simultaneously came Praveena's question, "How did these diverse events influence the course of Napoleon's destiny?"

Miss Krishnan broke into a broad smile. "So you girls have been attentive, after all. Very good. Now, before I tell you of the inseparable connection between the Revolution and Napoleon Buonaparte, I'd like you all to tell me of the last we saw of Napoleon, prior to the French Revolution."

"He had completed his studies."

"He graduated as a second lieutenant."

"He was only sixteen years."

The answers came in a medley of choruses, from varied sections of the classroom. When the excitement had settled down and silence reigned once more, Miss Krishnan resumed, "Correct. The last we saw of Napoleon was in the September of 1785, when, as a young lad of sixteen, he graduated as a second lieutenant of one of the foremost regiments of the French army. This was four solid years before the French Revolution. We shall now take up Napoleon's career from this point. Can you all take a guess where Napoleon was when the Revolution broke out?"

"France, serving the royal army," said one half of the class.

"Corsica, back to his homeland," cried the other half.

"Well, well. Let's see. Napoleon was appointed as an officer in the La Fere artillery regiment when we last saw him in 1785. The years 1785-89 were his apprentice years, where he trained as a military officer, and earned formal expertise in the nitty-gritties of artillery. As the second lieutenant of the regiment, he served his garrison duty at Valence and Auxonne, both communes in France."

"What is a commune, miss?" Samprada asked.

"A commune is the smallest administrative division in France."

"When the rebellion broke out in 1789, Napoleon took leave of the French army for a while and returned to serve the native shores. He became a fervent supporter of Pasquale Paoli, the Corsican leader who was pioneering the nationalist cause. In fact, Napoleon threw himself, heart and soul, in the political struggles of his nation. And for his peerless dedication and firebrand nationalism, Napoleon was rewarded heartily with vital military positions and promotions."

"Unfortunately for Napoleon, his own visionary dreams of Corsica's sovereignty proved to be his undoing."

"Why is that?" came the chorus, in askance.

"Napoleon's upward mobility was not well taken by Pasquale Paoli. Paoli perceived Napoleon's increasing popularity as a potent threat to his own position. The wary governor of Corsica sought for an opportune moment to square accounts with the overambitious youngster. And this came with their clash of ideals."

"Napoleon Buonaparte was quite content with the idea of a Corsican struggle as an integral part of the larger French struggle for independence. Pasquale Paoli, however, had other ideas. He envisioned a Corsica that was an independent nation in its own right. Paoli sought to break free from the French rule."

"The ever-widening chasm between the two leaders finally gave way, when the newly emergent French Republic extended the liberties of people of France to Corsica as well. Napoleon was thrilled. Paoli was not. The country was split into two hostile factions. One group whole-heartedly supported Paoli. The other pledged their fierce loyalty to Napoleon."

"A civil war finally erupted in the country wherein Napoleon was outnumbered. In June 1793, when Corsica gained its formal independence from France, Paoli had the entire Buonaparte family banished from Corsica on charges of treason. Ostracized (cast out) from his country as a traitor, the 24 year old Napoleon set sail with his mother and siblings to France; never, never again to step into the land of his forefathers."

A hush of silence came over the class, at this unexpected turn of events as every girl sat thinking - What did France have in store for the young hero?

Further reflections were cut short when the bell rang abruptly, shuttling them all back to reality; the reality of the next period, Mathematics.

Chapter 4

It had been a drab day for the students of 7 C. It had rained in the morning, and the students were in no mood for academics.

So when Miss Krishnan marched into the class for the fifth hour, and asked them instead, to fall into a single file and troop down to the school grounds, the girls let out delighted shrieks of excitement.

They assembled soon after in the open air auditorium. Savouring the fragrant whiffs of the breeze, the girls sat attentive to their teacher, who resumed the story without wasting even a moment.

"Napoleon Bonaparte was not a man to sit and brood over his past misadventures. Instead, the first thing Napoleon did upon reaching France was to embrace the more French version of his name. Napoleone di Buonaparte became Napoleon Bonaparte from thereon, and that's how history has recognized him ever since. Does that clarify your doubt now, Praveena?"

"Yes, miss."

"Napoleon now set himself to the strategic task of career-building. For this, he had to prove his mettle. His first opportunity came in 1793 when, as the artillery commander of the French Republican forces, Napoleon led the French troops against Toulon. Located on the Mediterranean coast, Toulon was the naval stronghold of southern France. However, a heavy military backing by the British had turned this city against her own government.

"Commissioned by the Republican government, Napoleon spearheaded the siege of Toulon. The enemy's bayonet had inflicted a ghastly wound on his thigh. But he staged a dramatic attack, expelling the British fleet from the harbour. Napoleon was rewarded with a promotion for restoring to the government what was a rightful French territory. Major General Bonaparte became Brigadier General Bonaparte at an astonishingly young age of 24."

Wonderstruck squeals of 'oohs' and 'aahs' filled the air. Even the teacher could not help smiling.

"Chill it, girls," said Miss Krishnan. "This is just the beginning of Napoleon's meteoric rise. We have a long way to go.

"Napoleon's next magnificent victory came in October 1795, when the government sought his help to disperse the raging Parisian mobs from the streets. These comprised mostly of French Catholic Christians who had been disgruntled by the anti-clerical or anti-church stance of the French Revolution and the First French Republic."

"Responding with lightning speed, Napoleon commanded his squadron to launch a fusillade of artillery fire on the mutineers. Within a matter of moments, more than 300 Royalist (pro-monarchy) agitators lay cold and massacred on the streets of Paris."

"The curbing of the Royalist insurrection proved crucial to Napoleon. An obscure general shot to fame overnight. Suddenly, wealth, fame, power, glory - all that Napoleon had aspired for - came to do his bidding. Napoleon became a national hero. He was designated Commander of the Army of the Interior. He was also given charge of the artillery segment of the Army of Italy."

"How can he be given charge of an army of another country, miss?"

"Oh, I am sorry. I should have been specific. By 'Army of Italy', I meant France's Army of Italy. In other words, it was a field Army that France had stationed at Italy. And from Napoleon's point of view, it was his first offshore military assignment."

"Do you all see now, how intrinsic the French Revolution had been to Napoleon's spectacular growth as a military commander?"

"Yes, miss."

"Good. We will move on to 1796, which was a significant year in Napoleon's life. Early, that year, on the 9th of March, Napoleon was married to Josephine de Beauharnais. She was the widow of a noble who had been guillotined during the Revolution."

"1796 was also the year when Napoleon's campaigns began to take a transnational magnitude. So far, Napoleon's movements had been confined to that of France, affecting only French interests. 1796 saw the emergence of a dynamic warrior and mastermind who was to shape the very destiny of continental Europe."

"Napoleon led a triumphant march into the city of Milan, Italy in 1796. He then declared himself as the president of a satellite government in Northern Italy, which he called the Cisalpine Republic."

"What is a satellite government, miss?"

"A satellite government refers to a state/country which is officially independent, but is under the powerful reigns of another controlling state/country. In this case, the Cisalpine Republic became a satellite state or client state of revolutionary France."

"Now, Napoleon did not stop with that. He also shipped to France, treasures worth millions of francs, looted in Italy."

"Napoleon's next target was the Austrians. After a series of whirlwind attacks, Napoleon effectively subdued Austria and constrained her to make peace. In fact, he dictated the very terms of the Treaty of Campo Formio (Italy) in October 17, 1797, by which France secured vast territory from Austria."

"It was a tremendous achievement. In just a matter of one and a half years, a single man had so inspired a whole bunch of shabby soldiers, down in the dumps of despair, to a robust battalion who ravaged the Austrian army without losing even a single battle."

"The Treaty brought a decisive end to the War of the First Coalition which revolutionary France had been waging since 1793 against the combined forces of Austria, Prussia, Great Britain, Spain and Sardinia."

"Napoleon then set off on a military expedition to Egypt."

Pat came the question from Samprada, "Miss, why did Napoleon go on a far-off crusade to North Africa? Were the French combating political enemies even in Egypt?"

"That's a very pertinent question," said Miss Krishnan, nodding approvingly, before she continued, "The political enemy that Napoleon was combating in Egypt was actually Great Britain."

"Great Britain?" cried fifty voices in disbelief.

"Yes. The War of the First Coalition had ended, no doubt. But there lurked an unvanquished enemy amongst the Coalition, Great Britain. Napoleon realized that if France was to establish absolute supremacy in the European subcontinent, she would first have to thwart Great Britain's ambitions of a similar dominance. Now, can any one of you tell me what the political situation in India was like, at this time?

A silence fell across the class, as each of them sat racking their brains for the parallel event, 250 years ago in their own country. The responses came in a murmur of phrases.

"The English East India Company."

Napoleon before the Sphinx, Egypt

"Divide and rule policy."

"Colonization."

"All right. You are almost there. If you remember well, this, this was about the time when the English East India Company had established itself in India after practically wresting out the French East India Company. This came as a huge setback to France's mercantile and colonial interests; and France did not take too kindly to it."

"Napoleon, the ace strategist, figured out a way to arrest Great Britain's growing supremacy. He decided to thwart Britain's emerging empire in India, by striking at her trade routes to India via the Mediterranean Sea. Now you girls tell me, where is Egypt located?"

Miss Krishnan gave a moment's pause, as she gauged fifty expectant faces, waiting for an answer.

"Put two and two together, girls. You know it."

Vaishali raised her hand slowly; half hesitating, half asking, "On the Mediterranean Sea?"

"There you are," Miss Krishnan beamed. "Egypt is located on south of the Mediterranean Sea. And Napoleon decided to handicap Britain's trade interests in India by crippling access on the Mediterranean Sea from Egypt."

"There was another reason too for Napoleon's choice of Egypt as a military destination. Napoleon knew that France did not possess sufficient naval power to take on Britain's Royal Navy in the English Channel; the channel which separated England from northern France. And hence, Napoleon proposed to undertake the expedition down south to Egypt. Now, is that clear?"

"Yes, miss."

"With pronounced intentions of establishing a French presence on the Mediterranean, Napoleon set forth to Egypt on May 1798 . The campaign, however, produced mixed results."

"As a military operation, the campaign proved to be a failure. Napoleon's fleet was routed out thoroughly by Horatio Nelson, the famous British admiral, at the Battle of the Nile in August 1798. Napoleon's dream lay quashed. But he did not let the imperial defeat on sea throw cold water on his personal ambitions."

"Aspiring for glory and name, Napoleon decided to conquer Egypt and Syria (on the east coast of the Mediterranean Sea) instead. Napoleon's military offensive on Syria failed to produce the desired outcome. Undeterred, Napoleon invaded Egypt. And, at the battle of Abukir on 25 July 1799, he completely devastated the Ottoman Turks, who held sway over Egypt at that time."

Prachi raised her hand, saying, "Miss, you said that the campaign was a failure as a military operation. But Napoleon's conquest of Egypt seems to have been a thumping success."

"I am only just coming to that, Prachi. The expedition was a military disaster, no doubt, but it did a whole lot of good to Napoleon's personal image."

Out burst a barrage of objections. "How is that possible?"

"Napoleon failed in the critical military operation against the British. Wouldn't the defeat have blotted his image to a certain extent?" another voice cried.

Miss Krishnan waited a few minutes before the excitement of the class died down. Then she said, "Well, Napoleon's expedition to Egypt was impelled not only by political necessity or individual motives. There was another reason too - that of cultural exploration."

"To the French people, Egypt was a land that held out the thrill of the unknown and the exotic. It had been the cradle of an ancient civilization - the land of the Pyramids and the Sphinx, the Pharoahs and the Mummies, the Nile and the Hieroglyphics, temples and valleys. So when Napoleon set out for Egypt, he took along with him not just contingents of soldiers thirsting for battle, but also a sizeable group of

Napoleon on his Imperial throne

French scholars - scientists, mathematicians, engineers, chemists, cartographers (mapmakers) - who came out with some dazzling discoveries. The foremost of these discoveries was the Rosetta Stone."

"The Rosetta Stone?" echoed the class in unison.

"Yes, a granite stone belonging to 196 BC that was found in Rosetta by the French scholars. The Rosetta Stone was a path breaking discovery. It was instrumental in understanding the cryptic hieroglyphics, something which no one had been able to decipher so far."

"Wow," exclaimed the fascinated class of 7 C.

" As you can all see for yourselves, the Egyptian expedition was an important cultural breakthrough."

"Napoleon returned to France in 1799. In November 1799, he engineered a coup d'état, a forced takeover of the government, to become the First Consul (head of the state) of a new three-member regime known as the Consulate. The power was now in his hands. He only needed to make some smart moves; which he did."

"First, Napoleon took up residence in the Tuileries Palace, home to the royal family of France until the French Revolution. Second, he redrafted the constitution such that it gave him tremendous dictatorial powers. Third, he amended the constitution in 1802 to become the First Consul for life. Finally, on December 2, 1804, Napoleon dissolved the constitution to coronate himself Napoleon I, the Emperor of France."

Even before the class could digest the staggering rapidity of the events, the bell rang, loud and shrill, to signal the last hour of the day.

Ah! And what a day it had been!

Chapter 5

It was a bright, crisp morning. The students of 7 C swarmed into their classroom in chatty clusters of twos and threes, after their Thursday morning session of Physical Training. There were ten minutes more for the bell to go.

But, hey, Miss Krishnan was already waiting in the classroom.

"Hurry up, girls!" said Miss Krishnan.

Within a matter of minutes, the students of 7 C had settled down.

"All right. Where did we stop in our last class?"

"Till Napoleon became the French Emperor."

"Fine. With the dawn of the nineteenth century, we step into the most important years of Napoleon's life and career. Here was, unquestionably, the most powerful man of France; the monarch of an empire at an incredibly young age of 35! And, he emerged as the prime architect of the political destiny of Europe, in the years to unfold."

"Now, there are two important aspects to his career from this point in 1800 AD. They are Napoleon, the aggressive imperialist and Napoleon, the monarch of France.

"The first quarter of the 19th century was marked by innumerable political conflicts amongst the European countries. France, in particular, had to combat the combined might of several European countries several times. These countries constantly formed multiple anti-French coalitions amongst themselves, because they were afraid that the anti governmental waves of the French Revolution would envelop their own countries, and threaten their very governments."

"War-ravaged France resorted to desperate measures to defend herself. For want of people to fight her wars, the Government enforced compulsory enrollment for military on her subjects. It also mobilized every available resource at her disposal for the sake of war."

"It was in this extremely fragile scenario that an artillery commander in France's Army of Italy was galvanizing thousands of dispirited soldiers into action. And when the War of the First Coalition came to an end, Napoleon Bonaparte emerged as France's beacon of hope. As time went by, Napoleon rose in the eyes of his people, as the spirited, dynamic hero that France needed in those chaotic times."

"Napoleon, on his part, kept up the overwhelming faith of the people in him. As a gifted military genius, he had done wonders by inspiring his men and boosting their morale; verily rekindling a nation's self-confidence."

"So far, France had been on the defensive; at the receiving end of the international attacks. But when Napoleon became the Emperor of France, he reversed the policy; adopting, instead, the offensive military posture. The first decade of the 19th century saw the meteoric rise of an emperor who led a series of aggressive military onslaughts against prominent European powers, to establish his supremacy over the European subcontinent. These came to be known in time as the Napoleonic Wars."

"So all his life, Napoleon only waged wars?" asked Vaishali, even as she thought to herself, "How unpleasant life must have been, all the time."

"Well, Vaishali, did he have a choice? Napoleon waged wars with European countries to strive for peace. But given the belligerent or warlike nature of his ambitions, he dictated terms of the very peace he strove to establish. The defeated country would accept those terms out of compulsion. But, in a short while, it would again ally itself with another European power and attack the French Empire. And so it went, on and on, like a vicious circle."

"Do you know that even as Napoleon returned from the Egyptian campaign, France was already facing a Second Coalition of Austria, Great Britain, Russsia along with minor European powers like the Kingdom of Naples, Portugal and the Papal States? It was Napoleon who took charge upon his return and restructured his military resources. With 40,000 men and ammunitions, Napoleon crossed the precarious St. Bernard Pass in the Alps mountain range, plodding through slippery layers of ice, into Marengo (Italy) to launch a surprise attack on the Austrians."

"It was an extremely daring initiative, which only a maverick like Napoleon could have taken. In the Battle of Marengo that took place on June 14, 1800, Napoleon's armies drove away the Austrians out of Italy. In the meantime in Germany, French forces under General Jean Victor Moreau had crossed the river Rhine to capture Munich (southern Germany) in the decisive Battle of Hohenlinden on December 3, 1800."

"The resultant of the War of the Second Coalition was the Treaty of Luneville (France), signed on February 9, 1801. By this treaty, the left bank of the Rhine River came to be mutually recognized as the sovereign possession of France. The treaty also reinforced the terms and clauses of the early treaty signed by the Austrians at Campo Formio in 1797."

"Napoleon also entered into an agreement with Pope Pius VII, in a bid to resolve the differences with Roman Catholic Church. This was the Concordat of 1801, which not only pacified the Pope and the Church, but restored order and peace within France."

"France had emerged triumphant a second time. If there remained a power to be contended with, it was Great Britain. Great Britain had almost always opposed France, and influenced a host of minor European powers to follow suit. Napoleon knew that for a long-lasting peace in the subcontinent, he would have to enter into a mutual peace treaty with Great Britain. This was the Treaty of Amiens (France), signed on March 27, 1802, which brought about peace in Europe, the first time in ten years!"

"Wow!" exclaimed the spirited class of fifty.

"Not just that, the treaty shot up France's admiration for Napoleon. The public assent was overwhelming. As for

Napoleon, he found this a perfect opportunity to encash upon to become the Emperor of France in 1804."

"Shortly on the heels of Napoleon's coronation came the murky clouds of war."

Samprada shot up her hand instantly. "But why would anyone wage a war when mutual peace had been agreed upon in the subcontinent?"

"It all boils to hostility and mistrust. And none the less to the overbearing dreams of continental dominance by the two European superpowers - France and Great Britain. Europe had not yet got over its scepticism of revolutionary France. And, the minor European powers had serious misgivings on the meteoric rise of Napoleon, the new upstart on the international scene. They could not bring themselves to trust his soaring ambitions."

"Irreconcilable differences had already broken out between France and Great Britain in 1803, regarding a disputed territory. Two years later, in 1805, the Third Coalition came into being, with Austria, Russia, and Sweden joining Great Britain in the fray, even as Spain aligned herself to France."

"Napoleon realized that France could never wage an upfront battle with the British on the seas and emerge victorious; such was their naval supremacy. He had marched along with 200,000 soldiers of his newly reorganised Grande Armee to Boulogne, on the very shores of the English Channel, in order to strike at Great Britain. And, then, much to the surprise of everyone, Napoleon unexpectedly asked his soldiers to turn homeward and ambush the Austro-Russian armies, instead."

"It was a strategy that had never failed him; an onslaught on the minor European powers, instead of tackling Great Britain. And it ended almost invariably in their disgracefuldefeat."

"Napoleon knew that the armies of the allied foes were scattered across the continent. Taking advantage of this situation, Napoleon's armies secretly advanced out of Boulogne, to attack the startled Austrian army at Ulm (Germany) from the rear, giving no time for the Russian soldiers under General Kutuzov to join the Austrians. 30,000 Austrian soldiers under Austrian General Karl Mack von Leiberich surrendered to the might of the French army."

"Meanwhile, the Royal Navy under British Admiral Nelson had dealt a devastating blow to the French celebrations by vanquishing the combined fleet of France and Spain at the Battle of Trafalgar (Spain) on the October 21, 1805."

"Unfazed by the debacle at sea, Napoleon proceeded with his troops along the river Danube to occupy Vienna, the Austrian capital, abandoned hastily by her emperor, Francis II."

"So did the war come to an end with Napoleon's occupation of Vienna, miss?" asked Prachi.

"Oh, no. Far from it. In fact, at this point of his conquest, Napoleon was in an acutely treacherous position. He had come a long way from Paris. His troops had dwindled and his supplies crippled. Napoleon could have chosen to sue for peace. But he still chose to declare war."

"On December 2, 1805, 70,000 French soldiers faced an allied army of 90,000 soldiers, personally led by the Tsar of Russia, at the Battle of Austerlitz. The outcome was decisive: the French army inflicted a crushing defeat on the Austro-Russian forces. That day, there was a dual celebration among French troops, for it was also the first anniversary of their emperor's coronation."

"The Battle of Austerlitz was Napoleon's finest battle; going down in military history as one of those unique campaigns in which a superior manpower succumbed effectively to the might of a superior military stratagem; a resounding victory of the brain over the brawn. In fact, the Arc de Triomphe, a monument that stands proud and impressive in Paris today, is a legacy of the Battle of Austerlitz. Napoleon got it built to immortalize the memory of the conquest."

"The War of the Third Coalition too came to an end with the signing of the Treaty of Pressburg (present Slovakia) on December 26, 1805. With this treaty, Austria was forced to cede strategic territories in the north of Italy to France, apart from paying a huge war indemnity (compensation) of 40 million francs."

"The most vital aftermath of the War of the Third Coalition, however, was the disintegration of the Holy Roman Empire."

"Where did this Holy Roman Empire suddenly come from, miss?" asked Praveena.

"The Holy Roman Empire refers to those provinces in Central Europe which came under the political control of the Holy Roman Emperor, ever since the Middle Ages. A Holy Roman Emperor was one on whom the Pope of the Roman Catholic Church conferred the title *Emperor of the Romans*. Francis II of Austria was the last Holy Roman Emperor. With his abdication, the Holy Roman Empire ceased to exist."

"Is it clear now, Praveena?"

"Yes, miss."

"Any questions, class?"

"Miss, you said that Napoleon invariably attacked the minor European powers, rather than confronting the British. So, did France ever have a chance to defeat Great Britain in an open battle?" The question came from Vaishali who was beginning to wonder why, despite having a military supremo like Napoleon, France had never seized a victory from Britain.

"Well, Vaishali, like I said earlier, Great Britain had a dominance over the seas which no European power could, at any point in time, equal."

"But what was it that France lacked, that it could never surpass Britain's naval supremacy?"

"Hmm. Interesting question. Visualize Britain in the world map. How does it look like?"

"Well, it is surrounded by the ocean on all sides."

"All right. And how about France?"

"France is a part of the mainland Eurasian continent. It does have vast sea coasts, but it is bordered by Germany and Spain on either sides."

"Good. When a country develops its defence forces, it strengthens its borders, isn't it? Great Britain is an island. It can be accessed only by sea. If you remember, we are only in the first decade of the 19th century, a good hundred years before the airplane was invented. So don't you think it made geographical sense that Great Britain had a really superior navy, in comparison to France, or for that matter, any other European power?"

The class was impressed. It was a whole new perspective.

"Napoleon knew this as well. And repeated failures at the hands of the Royal Navy had only strengthened his convictions. Napoleon also knew that his dream of a continental French empire would go unrealized if he did not come up with a long-term, practical solution to a solid foe like Great Britain. So Napoleon sought to consolidate by policy, what he could not accomplish by war."

"To start with, Napoleon established the Confederation of the Rhine in July 12, 1806 declaring himself as its Protector. It was constituted by 16 German states from the erstwhile Holy Roman Empire who leagued themselves with France as her satellite states. Later on, 19 other states joined the Confederation."

"The Confederation proved to be one of strategic politico-military advantages. It gave the French empire a backing of 15 million people (of the satellite states), thus fortifying France's defences on her east."

"But Napoleon, the shrewd statesman, didn't stop at that. He had to ensure that these 15 million people remained subservient or subordinate to his empire. He also had to retain his sphere of influence on those of his territorial acquisitions, which he had acquired by conquest, and which did not fall under the Confederation."

"So, Napoleon doled out principal territories amongst his brothers, appointing them rulers of their domains. The Kingdom of Naples went to Joseph Bonaparte. Louis Bonaparte was given Holland; and Jerome, the Kingdom of Westphalia. It was a brilliant political move, one that assured Napoleon dependability and non-resistance from these states."

"But, miss," piped in Samprada, "These measures only strengthened Napoleon's position in the east. How did they solve his problem of Great Britain in the west?"

"Napoleon came up with an ingenious plan to deal with Great Britain. This was the Continental System, by which Napoleon forbade the European nations from pursuing any sort of trade or commercial relations with Great Britain. Napoleon thought that if he could freeze the economy of Great Britain, she would be forced to buckle under and surrender to France."

"So did Great Britain yield, miss?" asked Vaishali.

The bell rang at this moment.

Miss Krishnan smiled. "What do you think happened?"

No response. Vaishali stood speechless and wondering.

"I will tell you tomorrow."

With these words, Miss Krishnan walked out of the class, a twinkle of merriment in her eyes.

Chapter 6

Friday morning. Vaishali waited impatiently for Miss Krishnan's class. So when the bell rang the third hour, Vaishali was besides herself with excitement.

Miss Krishnan strode in and nodded at Vaishali.

"Yes, my girl. So what do you think happened when France imposed the Continental Blockade on Great Britain?"

"Well, Great Britain struck back?"

"Precisely. Great Britain was not a country to yield hands down. France had attempted to stifle her economy and Great Britain would give her a fitting reply. This simmering hatred against France broke out in open aggression.

"In fact, even before Napoleon had declared the economic war on Great Britain, Prussia rose in rebellion against France."

"Why Prussia?" asked Prachi.

"Well, the rising number of the German states who joined the Rhine Confederation caused Prussia great dismay. She felt threatened for her future. Her fears gave rise to the War of the Fourth Coalition in 1806. The states who were party to this coalition were Prussia, Great Britain, Russia and Sweden."

"Napoleon, however, decimated the Prussians completely in the Battles of Jena and Auerstedt (both in present Germany) on October 14, 1806, and captured Berlin. Napoleon also forced the Russian army to strike the flag in the critical Battle of Friedland (Prussia). The outcome was the Treaty of Tilsit (Russia) in July 1807 by which Napoleon disposed of Prussia arbitrarily, to embrace a very strategic ally - Alexander I, the Tsar of Russia. Napoleon also founded the Polish state of the Duchy of Warsaw, from territories relinquished by Prussia."

"But, miss, Russia had opposed France twice - in the Wars of the Third and Fourth Coalitions. Why would Napoleon seek Russia's friendship?" asked Samprada.

"Russia enjoyed a natural predominance over eastern Europe, which Napoleon had to acquire in western

Europe by repeated conquests. By seeking a political ally in Russia, Napoleon dreamt of extending his sphere of influence over the whole of Europe. Russia, on her part, consented to be a part of the Continental Blockade against Britain."

"What Napoleon did not know then was that he had committed the two gravest blunders of his life - blunders that set the pace of his decline and hastened his speedy downfall."

"Blunders?" chorused an incredulous class.

"Yes, the unforgivable blunders of decreeing a wrong economic policy, and trusting the wrong political ally. You see, the Continental Blockade choked not just the economy of Great Britain, but also harmed the commercial endeavours of the other European powers, who felt they were being made scapegoats to Napoleon's imperialist ambitions. In these subordinated countries, there emerged, slowly but surely, a rising wave of 'anti-Napoleonic' nationalism. In the next few years until 1814, France would witness a series of parallel events that eventually led to the decay and demise of the Napoleonic Empire."

"Portugal was the first to cry foul, as she had thriving commercial relations with Great Britain. She refused to be a part of the Continental Blockade. So Napoleon, with his trademark streak of repressing defiance, captured Portugal in 1807."

"The occupation of Portugal sent waves of mistrust and antagonism across adjoining Spain. If Napoleon could occupy Portugal, what was the guarantee that he would not forcibly take over Spain? So the Spaniards thought. And bartering away their sovereignty to the ambitions of a menacing imperialist was something the Spaniards found unthinkable."

"But, miss," Praveena interrupted. "Hadn't Spain allied herself to France on earlier occasions?"

"No doubt, Spain had aligned herself to France in the War of the Third Coalition. But Napoleon was an ally then, desirous of their support."

"Well, Spain's fears proved well-founded. Under the pretext of reinforcing troops, Napoleon invaded Spain and replaced Charles IV, the ruler of Spain, with his brother Joseph Bonaparte in 1808. Napoleon simultaneously handed the reins of the Kingdom of Naples to his brother-in-law, Joachim Murat."

"Indignant at being placed at the mercy of a puppet ruler, the citizens of Madrid rebelled openly on May 2, 1808, slaying 150 French soldiers. In retaliation, the French army came down upon the Spaniards in the most barbaric and remorseless manner to set off what came to be known as the Peninsular War or the Spanish War of Independence. The battles were fought on the Iberian Peninsula, comprising of Portugal and Spain."

"The Peninsular War lasted for six years until 1814. It was one of the most brutal wars in history, with the French and the Spaniards slaughtering and mutilating each other by thousands. The War also saw the beginning of what came to be known in military lingo as guerrilla warfare."

"Gorilla warfare?" asked the amused class.

"No, guerrilla," Miss Krishnan smiled. Guerrilla warfare refers to a kind of military tactics in which small, concealed groups of combatants conduct surprise attacks and raids on the opponents. The opponents are thus caught unawares and are invariably defeated."

"But what does the term 'guerrilla' mean?" asked Vaishali.

"Guerrilla comes from the Spanish word 'guerra' or 'war', and means 'little war'. A striking feature of this kind of warfare is that the combatants are mostly armed civilians. It was just so in the Peninsular War, wherein large numbers of Spanish civilians took on the savage might of the French armies."

"Meanwhile, fresh hostilities in the east sought Napoleon's attention away from Spain. Napoleon sent constant reinforcements of French troops to keep the aggression going in his absence. Eventually, the French armies proved to be of no match to the spirited Spaniards, who were now aided by Portuguese and British troops under General Arthur Wellesley."

"With the stepping in of the British, Napoleon's dominance over the peninsula weakened. The war was leading France nowhere. But Napoleon clung on foolishly to its pursuit, determined to crush the will of the Spaniards. And that proved to be not just his undoing, but the undoing of France

"The 'Spanish Ulcer', as it came to be known, engulfed 300,000 of Napoleon's finest men. France incurred not just a tremendous loss of manpower and resources; she suffered a devastating blow to her morale from which she never ever recovered again. The imperialist dreams of Napoleon lay crushed before his very eyes."

The class sat awestruck and silent. It was a few minutes before Samprada could find her voice to ask, "Miss, which were the 'hostilities in the east' that demanded Napoleon's attention, right in the middle of the Peninsular War?"

"Well, that was Austria rearing her head once more inspired by Spain's fervent national struggle. She formed a fifth coalition with Great Britain in 1809. But Napoleon completely suppressed the Austrian armies at the Battle of Wagram (near Vienna, Austria) on July 5-6, 1809. The Treaty of Schonbrunn (Vienna) in October 14, 1809 between the two powers brought the War of the Fifth Coalition to an effective close, with Austria conceding substantial territories to France."

Praveena raised her hand. "Didn't Napoleon ever figure out a long-term solution for Austria, just as he had for Great Britain? After all, Austria played an active role in all the five wars of the coalitions."

"Napoleon did come up with a solution - an unusual matrimonial solution."

"But wasn't Napoleon married?" came the question from different quarters of the class.

"Yes, he was. But the matrimony that he proposed now with Archduchess Marie Louise of Austria was more of a strategic exercise in alliance-building. Archduchess Marie Louise was the daughter of Francis II, the Austrian Emperor. Napoleon hoped that the marriage would strengthen ties between France and Austria, and prevent Austria from fighting any more wars against France.

"There was another reason too. The Archduchess belonged to the House of Habsburg, which was one of the oldest royal dynasties in Europe. So Napoleon hoped that at least the heir born to his marriage with the Archduchess would be legitimately accepted by the monarchs of Europe, unlike himself, who was only an unknown Corsican upstart."

"The French Emperor was married to Archduchess Marie Louise of Austria on March 11, 1810. 'Aha! Peace at last!' - Napoleon might have thought then, but Providence had something else in store for him. Even as Napoloen cemented a new political alliance, a trusted older ally turned adversary."

"You mean Russia, miss?" Vaishali chimed in.

"Precisely. The repercussions of the Continental Blockade with Britain came to be felt in Russia. Burdened by an unsteady economy, Russia refused to comply with the lop-sided economic policy any longer. This was in 1811."

"Acutely let-down by Russia's withdrawal, Napoleon decided to raid Russia. His officers and counsellors advised him against the aggression. However, Napoleon was adamant. And, on June 24, 1812, he rallied over 600,000 soldiers from different soldiers of his empire, determined to repress the vast Russian country into submission."

"Fearing the onslaught of the French forces, the Tsar's army receded into the interiors of their country. The more the French army infiltrated, the more the Russian army retreated. The very retreating of the Russian forces cost Napoleon his very army."

"The Russian armies did not only just retreat within. Determined to leave nothing behind them - no traces of food or habitation, the Russian forces burnt the countryside as they marched along. Meanwhile, the excruciating summer of Russia had begun. Cut off from their home country, the French soldiers had to combat not just the gruelling heat of an alien country, but fatigue, disease, starvation and abandonment."

"Abandonment?"

"Yes. There were many non-French troops who were part of the army simply because their rulers owed allegiance to the French emperor. These were men who were stirred by no patriotic passions, and chose to desert the army midway rather than suffer sickness and death."

"Two months had passed. No battles had been fought. And Napoleon was already short of 150,000 soldiers!"

"Whooo!" came the gasp of amazement from the class.

"Finally, there was a single battle between the French and Russians at Borodino on September 8, where the Russian armies were routed. Still, the Russians did not officially surrender."

"On September 14, 1812, Napoleon and his triumphant troops marched into Moscow to capture it, only to have the biggest shock of their lives. Before them was an immense, terrifying conflagration, the likes of which they had never seen. Huge, gigantic tongues of flame darted out at them from everywhere. Moscow was burning."

"Burning?" asked the class in disbelief.

"Yes, it had been torched the night before by Russians, who preferred to set their city aflame rather than let it fall in the hands of the enemies."

"The Russians had wreaked a perfect vengeance. It was the peak of the Russian winter. The French troops were demoralized and war-weary. They felt the frosty bite of the icy, Siberian winds, even as the temperatures dropped sub-zero. The armies needed to halt their march for the winter. But the Russians had reduced to ashes the only place they could have put up for the winter's sojourn. The French troops had no choice but to trudge back to their country."

"The retreat of the French army was no carnival in the celebration of a triumph. It was a dance of death, of unrelenting defeat in the hands of nature. Left open in the freezing winter, Napoleon's soldiers fell one by one - of cold and starvation. Their horses died too, and the soldiers bickered and fought with each other for the horseflesh, to appease their hunger."

"If the want of food in a spiteful winter weren't enough, the French troops also had to face the cruel Cossacks, the Russian militant community who fell upon the debilitated army like a curse. The French invasion had wrought destruction upon Russia. In sheer vengeance, the Cossacks and the Russian peasants pounced mercilessly on the retreating French troops, sparing not even the ailing and the wounded. It was a bloodthirsty free-for-all that wrought a tragic end to the French soldiers. Of the 600,000 soldiers who began at the expedition, less than 20,000 remained fit for war."

The class sat in appalled silence, at the heartbreaking spectacle of countless soldiers dying in an unknown land.

Miss Krishnan paused a few seconds before continuing matter-of-factly, "Meanwhile, news reached Napoleon of an attempted coup at Paris. Abandoning his remaining troops then and there, Napoleon rushed back to take control of France."

"Renewed with hope and vigour at Napoleon's disgraceful retreat, the European powers came together, one last time in a majestic sixth coalition, comprising Austria, Great

Britain, Prussia, Russia, Sweden and several German states. The War of the Sixth Coalition began. Napoleon started out flamboyantly on a winning streak and defeated the combined forces of the Austrians, Prussians and the Russians in the Battle of Dresden (Germany) on August 16-17, 1813. It was to be his last decisive victory."

"In the momentous Battle of Leipzig (Germany) fought between October 16-19, 1813, the Allies inflicted a crushing defeat on Napoleon, to oust away the French control, east of the Rhine. The Battle of Leipzig was the largest battle in history prior to the First World War, and came to be known as the Battle of the Nations."

"Heavy-hearted and humiliated, Napoleon returned to France only to find himself despised by his people and boycotted by his marshals. They did not want to listen to him anymore. He had wreaked enough havoc with his reckless imperial ambitions."

"With Great Britain infiltrating from Spain and the Allies pinning down on him from Germany, Napoleon realized he was left with no choice. The Allies occupied Paris on March 1814. On April 11, 1814, by the Treaty of Fontainebleau (France), Napoleon abdicated as the Emperor of France to be exiled to the Island of Elba, (Tuscany, Italy). The Allies also restored Louis VIII (brother of the guillotined Bourbon ruler, Louis VI) to the throne."

"Napoleon, however, was not a man to be victimized by his fortunes. Even as the Allied victors deliberated over the restructuring of the vast French empire at the Congress of Vienna, Napoleon furtively escaped from Elba and reached France in February 1815. A regiment of soldiers blocked Napoleon's way, but upon seeing their good old general, they cheered him and marched him back to Paris, shouting all along the way, Long live the Emperor!"

"Upon reaching the capital, Napoleon rallied his forces one more time. But Providence had sealed his fate long ago. And in the historic Battle of Waterloo on June 18, 1815, the Allies led by Arthur Wellesley, the Duke of Wellington, defeated Napoleon a decisive, second time, banishing him to St. Helena, an obscure island in the South Atlantic Ocean."

"Napoleon's short, albeit dramatic return came to be known in history as the 'Hundred Days'. But with his exile to St. Helena, Napoleon would stage no more comebacks. Six years later, on May 5, 1821, Napoleon, the once Emperor of France died a few months short of 52; a disillusioned, lonely man."

The bell rang leaving the class in a state of flustered silence.

Chapter 6

It was Saturday and the last hour was Library. The class was abuzz with chatter. The civics teacher had left them early. One could sniff the holiday mood in the air.

When the bell rang, the girls leapt with joy. Amidst shrieks of excitement, the girls packed their bags and as they began trooping out of the class towards the library, Miss Krishnan walked in.

"Get back to your class, girls. I will be taking this hour."

Excitement dissolved into disappointment. Reluctantly, the girls shuffled back to their seats. Seeing their crest-fallen faces, Miss Krishnan said, "Come on, girls. I must complete the story. I need to resume my regular lessons at least from Monday, isn't it? I have already informed your library teacher. I will expect you girls to cooperate with me now, alright?"

"Yes, miss"

"Great. Now let me resume the story."

Prachi interrupted, saying, "But miss, you have already completed the story, isn't it, with Napoleon's exile and death?"

"Well, if you have paid close attention to my narration, there is one aspect to Napoleon's story which I haven't touched upon. Can any one of you tell me what is it?"

Pin-drop silence. As the class sat wondering, racking its brains, Vaishali ventured to speak, "Miss?"

"Yes, Vaishali?"

"You haven't told us about what Napoleon did for his people as a ruler."

"Very good. We haven't yet dealt with Napoleon as a monarch. We proceeded straight to Napoleon's campaigns on the international front. But we also need to learn what was happening on the domestic front. Because, a ruler is remembered by his people, not for the glorious wars he wages, but for the comprehensive reforms he brings about, to ensure their widespread happiness and prosperity."

"If we take a look at Napoleon's life, we find an emperor who was not merely a brilliant military commander but also an enlightened ruler. In fact, even before Napoleon rose to power, we find in him a man deeply influenced by the intellectual ideas of the Enlightenment."

"His Egyptian expedition is a case to the point. Like I told you before, Napoleon took with him an assortment of French scholars who studied the culture and civilization of Egypt. When Napoleon returned to France after the expedition, he found the Institutd'Egypte (Institute of Egypt) where these scholars established a data-base of their findings and generated some path-finding discoveries, including that of the Rosetta Stone."

"This was when he was only a military general, wasn't it, miss?" asked Praveena.

"Yes, before he seized power to become the First Consul. Napoleon's genius as a military general also lay in the widespread military reforms that he instituted once he came to power. The secret to France's consistent victories in the first decade of the nineteenth century lay in its invincible army, which had been reorganized and enhanced by Napoleon."

"The newly structured troops came to be known as Napoleon's Grande Armee. Napoleon organized them into corps. Led by a marshal or commander, each comprised of two or more divisions of 12000 men. These were only the infantry. In addition to these, they had a cavalry of 2500 men and their artillery units. They were also accompanied by the medical staff and supply carriage for ammunition and belongings. Thus, these corps were self sufficient mobile units; mini-armies by themselves, capable of keeping a battle on, till supplemented by more such divisions of corps."

"Notwithstanding corps, Napoleon personally directed a small, exclusive army known as the Imperial Guard. Apart from being self-contained like the corps, the Imperial Guard constituted of the most feared soldiers and war veterans, who could unleash havoc and terror in the opponent's armies. Napoleon used them mostly as a last resort, and when he did, the French victory was almost always certain."

"Were the French troops also equipped with special weapons, miss? You told us that the Battle of Austerlitz was a triumph of superior military stratagem over a superior manpower." Samprada asked.

"A very valid point, Samprada. If you remember, Napoleon was well-trained in artillery, placed right at the start of his career in an artillery regiment. No one could have known better than Napoleon the skilful use of sophisticated artillery and its potential."

"Thus, Napoleon introduced the use of mobile or self-propelled artillery to fortify his infantry. It was a pioneering move in his times, and gave his army the aggressive edge. Not just that, he standardized the measure and size of the cannonball in his artillery so that resupplies were easy and quick."

"More than anything else, it is the style of warfare that underwent a change under Napoleon. Under him, battles became more offensive than defensive. Napoleon was not content with merely putting up a spirited resistance against enemy infiltrators. He launched a bolder and a more aggressive mode of warfare. Napoleon initiated battles which were fraught with risks yet which believed in complete demolition of the opponent's forces.

"And he did this not just with the help of restructured manpower or remodelled artillery, but also with his innate flair for shrewd military stratagems. In fact, even today, military academies across the world study the war tactics and strategies which Napoleon put to brilliant use in his innumerable campaigns."

"But, these are only military reforms. How did they help the larger public, the civilians of France?" Vaishali interrupted.

"I was coming to that. Napoleon' reforms were confined not just to his soldiers but also to the citizens of France. He strongly felt that his people deserved a stability and peace, which had been denied to them by the long, uncertain years of the Revolution.

"With popular interest in mind, Napoleon embarked on the task of instituting administrative and judicial reforms. Significant among these was the Napoleonic Code enacted in 1804. The Napoleonic Code or the Code Civil, as it was known at that time, sought to establish the rule of law across France. It also attempted to secure for its people the Revolutionary ideals of equality before the law, freedom of religion and abolition of feudal privileges."

"Thus, for the first time in the history of France, there came to being a legal system that placed emphasis on written laws and accessibility across various segments of the society. Needless to say, the Napoleonic Code revolutionized the legal institutions across Western Europe."

"Apart from the civil laws, Napoleon also codified the criminal and commercial laws. The French Revolution and the recurrent international wars had drained the resources of the country. Napoleon, therefore, set about to secure the country's financial stability by bringing economic reforms through uniform taxation and currency."

"France's currency was known as the livre. But, after the Revolution, it came to be known as the franc. Napoleon standardized its value, across the country, to speed up economic stability. He then established the National Bank of France, which not just held inflation in check, but facilitated easy borrowing at feasible rates. Needless to say, the economy of France recovered to behold the sunshine of prosperity, the first time in many years."

"Napoleon next directed his energies towards education."

"Miss," asked Praveena, "Why would a monarch with aggressive imperial ambitions dedicate his time and efforts towards education? He had taken care of the vital areas of law-making and economy. Wasn't that enough for him?"

"Simple. Napoleon was a man who rose to power not because of his social standing but purely on the basis of merit. He knew what it meant to receive the gift of education the difficult way. So he wanted to make the liberating power of knowledge accessible to all. And as I've already told you, Napoleon was inspired by the principles of Enlightenment."

"Thus in France, under the Napoleonic rule, public schools were instituted, and these provided education totally free of cost. Higher education was made accessible to anyone who qualified on the basis of merit, regardless of one's religion or social status. Napoleon also patronized the arts and sciences and established academies for the advancement for the same."

"In fact, in May 1801, Napoleon even introduced the Legion d'Honneur. It was an order that officially recognized the meritorious achievements of an individual, civilian or military. That was Napoleon's esteem for merit. Even today, the Legion d'Honneur is the highest order of decoration in France, awarded to an individual who has distinguished himself by his services to his country, or the world at large.

"But the interesting thing about Napoleon's regime was the dual nature of Napoleon's government. Externally, it was a powerful centralized government, with carefully structured bureaucracy. But the undisputed fact remains that Napoleon's government was a success only because it enjoyed the overwhelming support of the people. The French populace had only just broken out of the shackles of a tyrant after the Revolution. But the very fact that they whole-heartedly accepted a monarchical rule under Napoloen speaks volumes for the national support that Napoleon enjoyed."

"Today, the very idea of a robust, centralized rule, which rests on the secure foundations of widespread public support has come to be known by the appellation *Bonapartism.*"

"Even today, the progressive reforms and legislation of Napoleon live on in the administrative and judicial structure not just of France but of Europe as well."

Vaishali was delighted to discover that Napoleon wasn't a self-centred, ambitious emperor, after all. "So, as a ruler, Napoleon was just and liberal, wasn't he, miss?" she piped in.

"Well, Vaishali, Napoleon, the man was a bundle of contradictions. He was a despotic monarch, who often disregarded wise counsel, yet he was a benevolent ruler concerned with public welfare. He esteemed merit and calibre in people, yet he utilized his talent in making his way up the social ladder, to serve his selfish, personal ambitions. He was also a self-driven workaholic, who would proudly say - *Power is my mistress.*"

"Napoleon did have his failings, no doubt - over ambition and recklessness, and an arrogance that believed it could do no wrong. In fact, he always believed that he had been chalked out for a glorious destiny. What made him great was that he did not rest merely on his words and beliefs but strove to create that destiny."

"Yet, few could equal Napoleon in tact, planning and statesmanship. He was not only a peerless military genius, but also an administrator non-pareil. Napoleon's story was, indeed, one of Ambition capitalizing on History (the French Revolution, in his case), and combining that with Merit, Opportunity and Hard Work to rise to great heights."

"Napoleon was also one of those unique leaders who determinedly led his soldiers by example. He was right there leading the frontal attack in any battle rather than commanding his soldiers from a sheltered citadel or alcove. In fact, Napoleon shared a boisterous relationship with his soldiers and generals. They, in turn, affectionately referred to him as *Le Petit Corporal* or *The Little Corporal.*"

"Little Corporal?" asked the amused class.

"It may interest you all to know that Napoleon was a man of short stature. History ascribes to him a height that was a little below average."

"Hey, that's cute." This came from Preethi, the towering back-bencher.

"Yes. But see what heights of eminence Napoleon rose to, purely on account of his calibre and hard work. And here, I believe, is a lesson for all of us. One must never judge a person by his physical appearance or stature, nor feel diminished because of it. Ultimately it is one's individual merit that takes a person to glorious heights.

"The charismatic life of Napoleon embodies this lesson for us. Here was a rare individual who took history in his hands and steered the political destiny of an entire continent in the first decade of the 19th century. His tremendous impact on society and economy, culture and science was felt not just in the France of his times but even until the present day. And that, I believe, is Napoleon's irrefutable legacy to the world."

"All right, girls. Before I forget, the auditions for the ballet on Napoleon will be held in the Language Lab on Monday after school hours. Those of you who want to participate in the ballet must report to the Lab sharp at 3 o' clock. And please inform your parents beforehand about your late timings. Is that clear?"

"Yes, miss" came the vibrant chorus of fifty.

"Good. You may pack up now," so saying, Miss Krishnan walked out of the classroom.

Napoleon

The resonant peals of the school bell sent shrieks of jubilation across the classroom. The class of 7 C sprang on their toes in excited anticipation of the weekend ahead. Even as they swarmed outdoors, jabbering and giggly, a little girl in the class strode out alone, confidence in her step and a song in her heart. That day, she had the biggest smile of them all.

Two Months Later...

The French Festival at the Carmel Convent School was a rip roaring success. Accolades poured in especially for the ballet, and the stellar performance of Vaishali who played Napoleon.

The Alliance Francaise of Pondicherry had been so impressed with the ballet that they requested the school principal to send the ballet troupe to New Delhi to perform at the Golden Jubilee celebrations of the Alliance Francaise de Delhi, a month later; to which she only happily agreed.

Our girl became a star overnight. Senior students often dropped in by 7 C to take a look at the famous little new comer.

A few weeks later, Vaishali got down from the school bus and marched into the lobby. It was a regular day at school. Even as she walked in lost in her thoughts, a classmate thumped her back with gusto crying, "Hey Petit Corporal! Dreaming away to glory, huh?"

Vaishali smiled, a warm, radiant smile, in response.

It was fun being short, after all.

Prodigy books

Biographies

- Abdul Kalam
- Charles Darwin
- Marie Curie
- Visvesvaraya
- Srinivasa Ramanujan
- Newton
- Einstein
- James Watt
- Sir JC Bose
- Alexander Graham Bell
- Gandhi
- Jawaharlal Nehru
- Mother Teresa
- Ambedkar
- Bhagat Sigh
- Tipu Sultan
- Rani of Jhansi
- Akbar
- Shivaji
- Bharati
- Rabindranath Tagore
- Martin Luther King
- Alexander the Great
- Napoleon
- Adolf Hitler
- Charlie Chaplin
- Walt Disney
- Bill Gates
- Narayana Murthy
- Columbus

Classics Retold

- Homer's Iliad
- The Odyssey
- The Tempest
- Hamlet
- The Merchant of Venice
- Twelfth Night
- Romeo and Juliet
- Macbeth

Other Titles

- The Universe
- Hinduism
- Global Warming
- Abraham Lincoln
- The New 7 wonders of the World
- Life
- Tsunami
- Dinosaurs
- Ganga
- World War II
- Madras - Chennai
- Exam Tips
- Television
- Effective Communication
- Creative Thinking